7 STEPS TO CREATE IMPACTFUL ONLINE COURSES

Blueprint to course design, promotion, profiting and worldwide success

Dionisio Gonzalez C.

To all my students all over the world,

for making the difference.

INTRODUCTION

Online courses are becoming a booming industry all around the world, with estimations to surpass the 300 billion dollar mark by 2025, they also represent an excellent passive income idea to profit from your knowledge in a particular subject.

Teaching online have become one of the most gratifying experiences of my life, being able to reach thousands of students in more than 60 countries and 13 languages. The technique i'm about to share with you has made possible to create over 20 online courses with worldwide reach.

See your students' locations and languages

| 🌐 63 countries | 💬 17 languages 🌐 |

It is therefore due to my teaching passion that i want to share with you my approach to course creation and open the possibility for you to profit from this industry using your own personal set of skills. I want to make clear that this book is not a "secret recipe" or other cliché compilation of information, it is a blueprint for effective course design and to becoming prolific in several subjects.

Many online teachers create one or two course and then face a problem of flatenning and finally stop developing more courses, other teachers face stage fright with thoughts like: "I am not an expert.", "What if this doesn't work?" and never start at all, this book is specially directed to this teachers to help overcoming these fears, everybody is good at something and with the appropiate approach may turn into an expert or provide an online community of students with some level of expertise.

Procrastination is a mental block holding you back. You have to acknowledge your feelings so you can replace the negative thought with a positive one. The reality is that no technical skills are required to use a course platform and you can start without any monetary investment.

So there is virtually anything holding you back to start this path to provide value to a community throught online teaching, being able not only to profit from a particular skill but to become prolific in many different subjects and..a worlwide success!.

* * *

SELECTING THE SUBJECT

First Step: Defining the scope of the course

One of the most crucial stages of creating your online course is to select the subject and characteristics of the classes, you need to select subjects that are both interesting and profitable, it is crucial that is a topic in which you can gain proficiency in short time.

This first step is the most difficult to do, because it requires a lot of investigation and will to start, doing some market research and investigating is proven to be the hardest part of online course design.

The course selection criteria is similar to this:
a) A subject in which you are knowledgable or able to gain proficiency fast
b) It inspires you to investigate (passionate)
c) Profitable

This means the 3 columns for course topic selection are:

Knowledge: You are an expert (or can become an expert) on a certain topic, it can be because your education (degree or certificate) or because of practical knowledge on the subject. I have found useful to include practical cases from both my education or practical knowledge, by doing this the student gets in insight on the application of the knowledge.

Passion: It is demonstrated that passion influences your performance, some saying by +30%, passion is that internal force that push you to do something, passion alone will not do the work, it needs to be associated with discipline and constant work, the fact that you are reading this lines means that you have both characteristics because you are investigating on a subject to become better in the subject. Small actions surely make the difference! Online courses might be your calling and where you can succeed and give back to the community.

Profitability: This is the easiest factor, for your course to suceed you need one thing: students! To get this students you must solve a problem throught your knowledge. People are struggling with everyday subjects and even the smallest of tasks could be extremely difficult for those who aren't knowledgeable enough in a particular area (i.e talking french, raising fish in an aquarium).

Having these 3 factors in mind will help you at the moment to select the subject of your course. Now that we have established the main columns or characteristics to start designing the course we can start (action!) by:

1) Brainstorm Your Idea
In this initial stage you don't need to have the full picture of the course, you must make a deep search in which you have to evaluate the knowledge or skills you have developed in your work/career or subjects in which you can gain proficiency fast, for example, if you are a civil engineer you might be able to learn computer assisted design (CAD) since it is related to the field or if you are a chef you might be good at peruvian cuisine if you practice

for example.

Hobbies that you are passionate about: it's easier and more enjoyable to teach people on a subject that fascinates you and have a passion for instead of doing something just for the sake of it.

Think if you have ever coached somebody in a certain subject. That topic might be a good start for course development.

Think about your personal history and evolution, each one have a powerful story to tell, me, for example had to overcome a very limited childhood in one of the most dangerous cities in the world (Caracas), then go to a public college to obtain an engineering degree, the adversities in my life pushed me to search different income generating ideas (from which i eventually created courses to help other people) and to learn 4 languages (English, Spanish, French, Portuguese) to easily communicate my ideas all over the world and reach billions of people at a time. Everybody have a story to tell, from my own i have created over 20 courses and at the moment of writing this book i'm planning to create 4 courses dedicated to learn foreign languages.

Take into account a personal transformation you have been through: every person carries their own experiences, what helped you cope through a difficult time of your life? And what have you learnt from it? If this lesson can be used to help others overcome the same problem you can design an online course for it.

2) Research Your Course Idea

People join courses because they want to gain academic or transferable skills in their career, longterm learning or because they want a career change or diversify income source.

Among the inscription cathalists (accelerators) we find that people want to learn from a person that inspires trust, experienced and with authority in the field. They want to have access to information that is easy to digest and follow. They want to have a clear and measurable outcome.

Ask yourself in your course idea fulfills this parameters, match these with your current knowledge and the possibility of creating great content in the subject.

You can always perform an online search for the most successful courses, many marketplaces like Udemy, Coursera or Skillshare post information and data of the most popular courses. Some of the main course topic ideas include:

Programming: Python, C++, Web development, Java, Programming Languages, Video game programming.

Business: Forex, Data Science, Stock trading, Project Management, AI, blogging, Marketing, Presentations, leadership, podcasting, real estate, accounting, online business.

Finance: Bookkeeping, Blockchain, Trading, Financial Math, Investment Banking, Personal finance, passive income, Tax Preparation.

IT: Linux, Network security, Ethical Hacking, Cyber Security, Cisco CCNA.

Office Productivity: Microsoft Word, Excel, PowerPoint, SharePoint, Data Modeling, Data Visualization, Mac Basics, SAP.

Personal Development: Memmory, Parenting, Learning strategies, self development, Life Coaching, coaching, branding.
Design: Photoshop, Adobe Illustrator, 3D Modelling, AutoCAD, WordPress.

Marketing: Digital Marketing, Social Media Marketing, Google

Analytics, Content Marketing, SEO, Email Marketing, Affiliate Marketing.

Lifestyle: Watercolour Painting, Cooking, Wine, Cookie Baking, Cake Decorating, Bartending, Beaty, Cosmetics, Skin Art, Nail Art, Hair art.

Photography: Image Editing, Digital Photography, Colour Grading, Videography.

Health/Fitness: Weight loss, CBT, Home Workout, Nutrition, Massage, Dieting.

Music: Guitar, Music Theory, Music History, Music Production, Piano, Singing, Songwriting, Music Composition, DJ.

Teaching & Academics: English Literature, IELTS, Online Course Creation, Foreign Languages, English Grammar, Math.

I'm sure you are good in at least one of this activities, you just need to select in which topic do you think you can solve problems and add value with your courses.

3) Refine Your idea

Think about what is the purpose behind your idea and what problem does it solve and get down to specifics. Work in what will make your course unique.

It is always a good idea to niche your audience, be ask specific as possible: is your course useful to your audience? Is it providing value to the student? Is it unique? What is the level of experience, are they beginners or experts?

As you did on the course theme you can also search the appropiate audience by searching online. Reading through comments, questions, problems and reviews can give you a quick way into your audience's thoughts.

Try looking at the following:

- Facebook groups
- Quora questions
- Reddit results
- Amazon book reviews

Find out where your potential students "hang out" where they express the information they need, problems, questions, etc. Some of the online sources are forums, blog discussions, facebook groups, quora questions, reddit

Building a successful online course can be summarized in: Find a pain, problem or desire and design an online course that offers the solution

4) Research the Competition

If you have competitors that's good. It means there is demand in the industry and that is a good subject to develop into a course. Or maybe you are about to become a competitor in a main field, if this is the case, your course needs to be different, offer a simpler, cheaper or more effective solution to the student's problems.

The acquisition of skills and knowledge in online learning can cover a range of subjects covering from soft skills to technical skills or very specific ones covering custom-made online courses. To ensure that the subject you choose is a good subject, find out if someone else has done it before you. These procedure has helped me to create several courses in many subjects of interest:

Professional guide for Digital Painting with Krita

LIVE $99.99 - Public

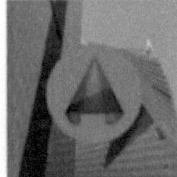

Autocad Civil 3D: Guia completa y casos practicos

LIVE $199.99 - Public

Geospatial Data Analysis:Introductory GIS and Remote Sensing

LIVE $199.99 - Public

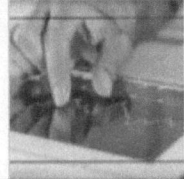

Professional Guide for Dividend Investing

LIVE $69.99 - Public

❊ ❊ ❊

PERFECTIONATE YOURSELF

Step 2: Become an expert in the field

C hoose an industry that you find deeply interesting and then dedicate the time necessary to become an expert in the field or gain a significant level of proficiency.

Pick a career at which you have some talent. Talent is the aptitude for the subject and the ability to improve in the long term.

Although practice is a huge portion of the equation, a person who doesn't have an aptitude for science is unlikely to become an expert physicist for example.

Engage in "deliberate practice." constant practice requires you to challenge yourself with difficult tasks in your field, rather than simply practicing at your current level. Some experts say that 10000 hours of practice in a subject can become you an expert in a certain subject. Once you are comfortable with your level in the field then you can start to elaborate the course or courses. Remember that students want to receive information from people they trust and that are seen as experts in the area.

The practice period will vary greatly depending upon the subject. For example, it takes approximately 800 hours to become an expert at Tai Chi and over 40,000 hours to become an expert cardiologist.

Read industry books. Back up your experience with study and research. Stay current on the newest trends in your industry. Be a creator of this new trends!
Learn from the current experts, not only the technical part bur also the educational techniques. Enroll in classes, conferences and certifications to support that you have learn from trustworthy sources.

Gain proof of your expertise (master or doctorate degrees, executed projects, conferences, certifications, testimonials), this will help you to market your hability and authority in the field.

Start your own blog. Throw out expert advice. Become a guest blogger. Contact other industry blogs and volunteer to do an occasional blog on their site. Optimize your blog for social media. So that your work can be found and followed.

Look for openings at your local university or Learning Center. Learning to teach your expertise is essential for selling yourself as an expert consultant.

You can also post your own video classes on YouTube or Vimeo. Post them to your blog as "expert advice." When trade conferences start asking you to speak without an application, you will know you are recognized as an expert (Don't forget to monetize this expertise).

* * *

STRUCTURE YOUR COURSE

Step 3: Organize the course content

F ocus On The Big Picture. You don't need to create 20 the-orical videos to have a great course. Remember the reasons that push students to enroll in a course: they want to learn from an actual person with experience, the information is put together in an easily digestible step by step system.

If a course section can create a measurable outcome, progress or transformation then it must stay in the course structure other-wise don't include it.

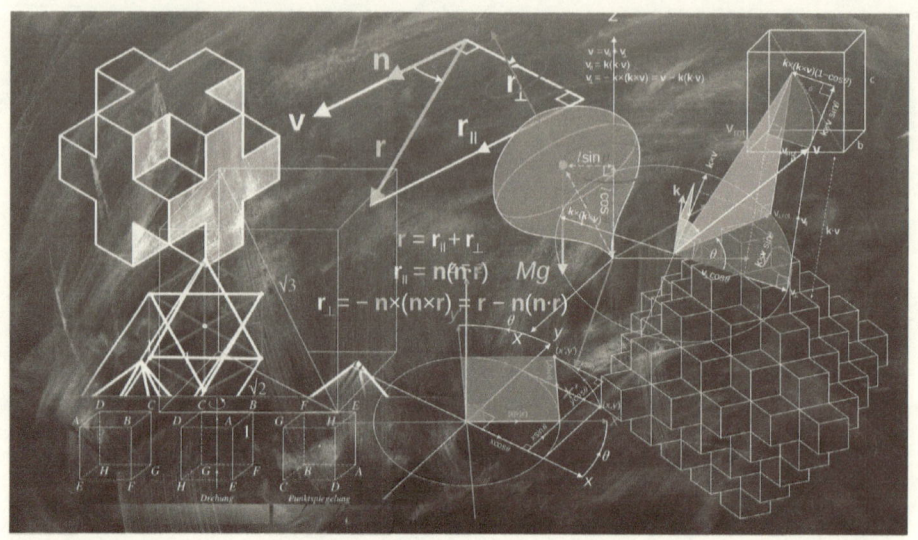

Your course should deliver your students to the main outcome or transformation in the simplest and quickest way possible.

Online Course Format
There are 3 main formats that you could use as a basis for your online course structure:

1) A step by step program
2) A week by week program
3) A reference course

I generally select a reference course with an initial section for understanding the technical lingo or "slang" of the specific course. 50% of a a learning process consists in mastering the lenguage of the subject, then the other 50% consist in knowing the application of what you just learned.

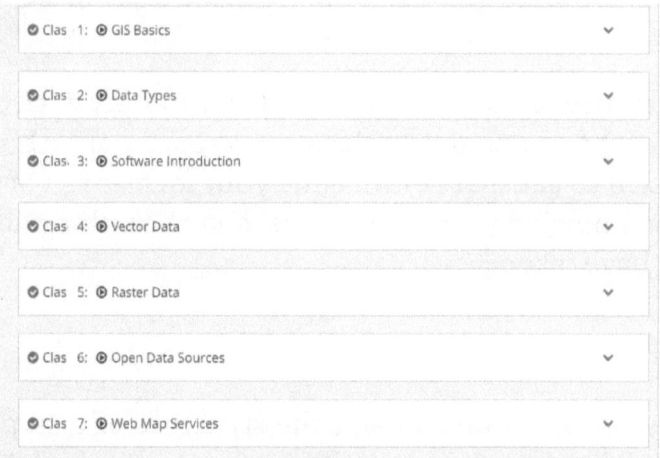

This is an example of a GIS course, notice the first section is oriented in mastering the theory of the subject. Each step builds on the previous one, working in a logical sequence towards the end, where the goal is accomplished.

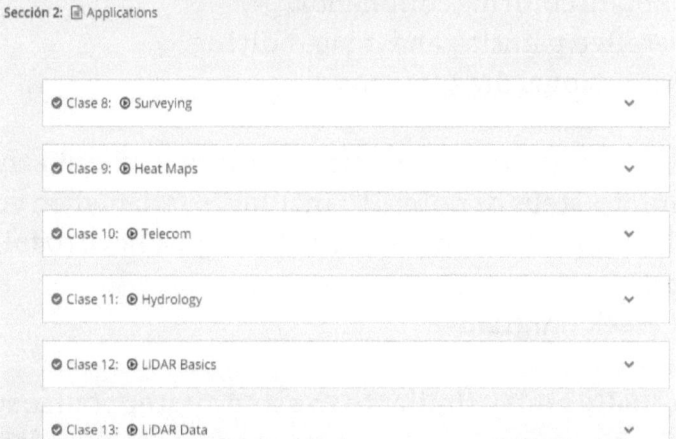

For the final section we have practical applications of what we learned in the initial stage of the course. Some classes come with a homework project.

Step by step courses

Each module or step will then contain a number of lessons within it that teach the actual content. Breaking it up into a handful of key modules is just a simple way for your students to recognise the main stages they'll move through as they reach their outcome.

To arrive at an outline of these steps, you can start with the main outcome of the course and work your way backwards through the steps needed to get there or imagine your former self before you gained the knowledge you now have, and then plot out the key steps you have taken.

An Example

The perfect way to understand the structure of a step by step course is with an example, let's think of a course called "5 steps to master photoshop" with a structure as follows:

Step 1: Describe the software outline and general commands
Step 2: Explain drawing commands
Step 3: Explain coloring commands
Step 4: Detailed painting and image editing
Step 5: Professional drawing tips

For each key step in your course outline, you should then draft the key micro-steps or points to include, so that when you come to actually make the course material, you just have to follow this framework.

Week By Week Program

This is actually pretty similar to the step by step course structure – the main difference is just that your course is organised over a specific time scale, with modules and lessons for each given week of the program.
For example, you might have an 8 week guitar course or a 4 week italian course.

It enables you to teach a process that will take a specific amount of time to learn or complete, and gives your students a chance to carry out tasks each week alongside. This approach doesn't work so well if what you are teaching is more conceptual.

Reference course

A reference course is a collection of knowledge and information bundled neatly together and well organised, which people can refer to relevent sections of whenever they need.

Often the info in a reference course might already be out there for free on the internet, but in a disorganised and low quality way.

By pulling it all together in one place and teaching it in a clear way, you create real value and help to solve people's problems.

Now that you know the different types of online course it is time to apply the format you find more suitable for the subject you selected and from there on creating the structure per se:

IDENTIFY YOUR CUSTOMERS STARTING POINT

IDENTIFY THE RESULT YOUR CUSTOMERS WANT TO ACHIEVE. This is basically the "promised land" or the main goal of your course. It could be anything from having a happier marriage, starting a successful business, becoming an amazing public speaker, or achieving their ideal body weight.

IDENTIFY THE ACTIONS YOUR CUSTOMERS NEED TO TAKE TO REACH THE END RESULT

IDENTIFY THE INFORMATION YOUR CUSTOMERS NEED TO KNOW IN ORDER TO TAKE THE REQUIRED ACTIONS. From there, we can determine what your customers need to know in order to complete these actions.

IGNITE ACTION

The only way your customers even have the chance of reaching those results is if they implement what you teach. Include resources that make taking action easier such as worksheets, checklists, cheat sheets, and step-by-step guides.

BUILD IN STICK STRATEGIES

o Providing quizzes at the end of each module
o Giving users assignments to complete before being able to move on to the next module
o Weekly live q&a sessions

INCORPORATE ENGAGEMENT AMPLIFIERS

o Badges for completing activities, lessons or courses
o Points Awarded
o Leaderboards
o Private Facebook group
o Bonuses for reaching a certain number of points.
o Course Progress tracking
o Public Recognition

* * *

CLASS CREATION

Step 4: Generate the videos and course classes

I t is time to generate the classes of the course, all the content must be oriented into solving a problem, always have this goal in mind when generating the content

Plan your presentation – step away from your computer
Step away from the keyboard. Pick up your notes and plan out the key points that you will make to help your audience take in your message. Then add a story or anecdote for each point. Although most academic presentations need to contain facts and figures, it's the stories and emotional connection that we remember and connect with.

Create your visual aids – and keep text to a minimum
Look for images that support your points and stories. You can find plenty of free-to-use photos by searching online (i.e Pixabay). Best of all would be to use your own photos.

You may be required to use a academic template. Ensure the images you use are consistent with the style and colour scheme.

Consider your use of text carefully. Use text sparingly and use a large, clear font. It can be useful for quotes or to emphasise a point that you've just made.

Rehearse – keep to time
Practice will make you better. Rehearse what you're going to say and how you're going to use your slides. The rehearsal process builds confidence and also allows you to practise your timing.

Always check what equipment you'll need to use when recording

(In the next chapter i will be talking about the equipment also)

Deliver your powerful presentation – Smile
Take a deep breath. Smile while you are recording (there is a difference when you talk smilying). Then enjoy the experience of delivering your powerful presentation to an audience that will be enthralled, delighted and convinced by your message.

* * *

LAUNCHING YOUR COURSE

Step 5: Select a platform to host your course

O nce your course is done you have left the educational part and entered in the business part of the process. The next step is to decide where to host your course. In this chapter we are going to evaluate some of the best options on the market

THINKIFIC
Thinkific's mission is to power your education empire. They are one platform with a robust set of user-friendly features, email marketing tools, membership site integration for your lessons, and excellent 24/7 customer support.

TEACHABLE
You can choose to use the online course platform for free (with $1 + $0.10 for all transactions) or select one of their three plans ranging from $29/month to $399/month.

LEARNWORLDS
The first step is creating the look and feel of your online course with their custom landing and sales pages. You can use their library of responsive templates and styles to build your course site and even add additional information pages.

KAJABI
It features powerful course site themes, robust email marketing automation, upsells and digital products, a customizable checkout, and blogging functionality.

LEARNDASH
LearnDash is an online course platform that integrates with WordPress. Some big websites using LearnDash include Yoast, Infusionsoft, the University of Michigan, and WP Elevation.

PODIA
Podia allows over 11,000 users to create, host, and sell their lessons with one easy-to-use platform. There are no transaction fees, and a simple three-step process has your course website up in no time.

RUZUKU
You can quickly create course outlines, edit and reorder your steps with ease, launch your course, and generate sales in no time.

ACADEMY OF MINE
A standard feature of any plan is completely free development hours to help set up and launch your course with customized integrations.

WIZIQ
They provide the latest tools for live training such as discussion boards, video streaming, mobile options, assessments, and analytics.

SKILLSHARE
Skillshare is a large marketplace focused on creative education. Topics include anything from graphic design and music production to fine art and cooking.

UDEMY
Udemy is one of the best online course platform marketplaces with over 24 million students, 35,000 instructors, and unbelievable 80,000+ courses.

TREEHOUSE
They feature 300+ technical courses on coding and development, over 50,000 students, and over 27,545 minutes of video.

LINKEDIN LEARNING
LinkedIn Learning is another online course marketplace tailored to business professionals. With over 1,000 business courses on topics like project management, web development, and digital marketing.

COURSERA
Coursera is a professional online course marketplace with virtual classes from some of the world's best companies and universities like the University of Michigan, Duke, and Stanford.

* * *

PROMOTE YOUR COURSE

Step 6: Learn how to market your course

S oftware and equipment are required to create high-quality content. However, you don't need the most expensive, high-end equipment to get started

Microphones are crucial. Bad audio is much easier to detect than shaky video, and you need a quality microphone for your course to sound excellent. Use the best microphone you can afford.

Having a good set of noise-canceling headphones will help tremendously during the editing process. They also come in handy when conducting interviews and recording someone.

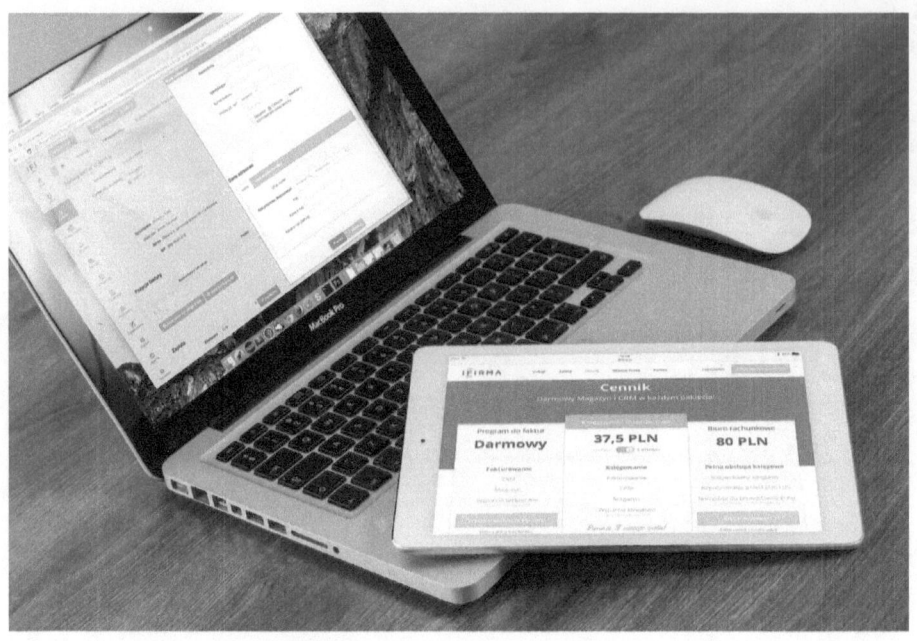

If you're creating a class on a piece of software or computer program, you'll have to show the screen to highlight the work you're doing.

Once you're done shooting your course, the real magic happens with editing.

Quality three-point-lighting is crucial to ensure your instructor shines Create compelling video courses. Use video plus interactive worksheets, PDFs, quizzes, and other elements to engage.

TAKE TIME TO MARKET YOUR BUSINESS
Although most online platforms promote your courses it will behove you to do some promotion by yourself (this ensures more percentage of the profits), direct publicity is not always the best, community building and reference are always the best approach.

Build a social media following. Create your own Facebook Business page so that you can engage with your community. Share your latest updates on Twitter and Instagram. Having a regular post schedule and providing engaging social media content will help build a community behind your brand.

Provide links of your courses in video sites such as YouTube, or Vimeo, answer related questions in Quora, Build a landing page and direct Facebook traffic (organic or paid) to this course Landing Page

HAVE CONTROL OVER YOUR BRAND.

You should be able to set your pricing and policies, incorporate your logo, and make the experience consistent with your business.

DELIVER AN EXCEPTIONAL LEARNING EXPERIENCE.

The platform should deliver a great learning experience. You should include multiple content types like audio, text, documents, and more.

INTEGRATE WITH OTHER TOOLS.

Choose a platform that integrates well with other solutions. You're going to want to make sure your learning platform can work with other tools like email marketing services, analytics solutions, and more.

LEVERAGE CUSTOMER SUPPORT

The platform should offer excellent customer support and training. A lot of services offer free resources and training, a dedicated account manager, and a helpful instructor community that can help you succeed.

* * *

RESEARCH & REPEAT

Step 7: Create multiple courses

T he best value your students can ever get is from a community. Although learning is somewhat of an individual activity, it is still a social process.

By building a community around your online course you're helping your students become self-sufficient and rely on the group.

Once you've got the community settled then you have access to direct information from your current students regarding which other course they would like you to develop.

Student demand for English courses on **Virtual Machine**

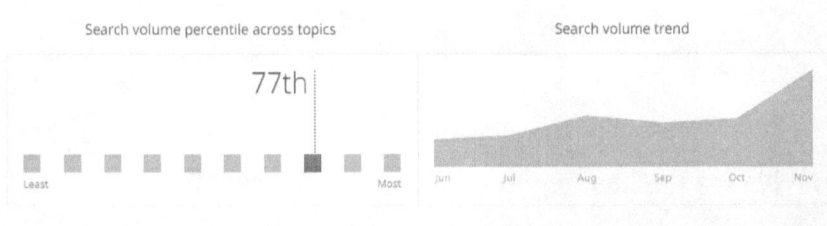

Creating the first course is always the hardest part, after this stage you can research for other related terms and how well are they doing (application of steps 1 and 2 of the guide), for example in the image above we have searched virtual machine volume search, with this information i can decide whether or not it is advisable to create a course in this area.

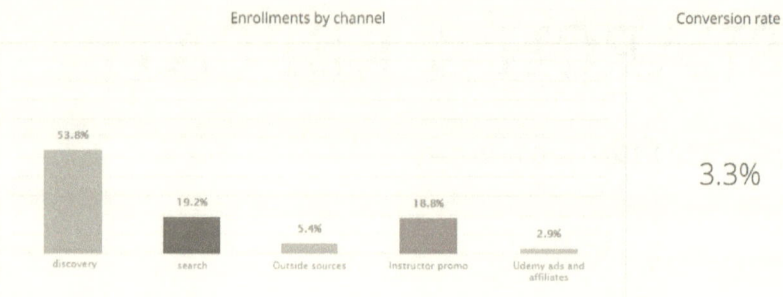

You can also monitor your current courses on how well they are doing to have an idea from where your traffic is coming and increase your marketing efforts in that direction, also you can ask for feedback to increase your conversion rate.

The key is to monitor, direct efforts towards effective marketing, increase profits for existing courses. On the other hand, search in the marketplace for promising subjects (search volume, conversion rate, highest rated competition, etc) and repeat the process learned in this book to create all the quality courses that you wish.